Clicker Training

Katharina Schlegl-Kofler

Contents

52 Help with Problems

Clicker Basics

Would you like to train your dog in a way that makes practice fun for you and your pet? Then clicker training is one good way to achieve your goal. Once you become familiar with it, you will discover many ways to keep your dog actively engaged.

Clicker Training—Fun for Human and Dog

For some time clicker training has enjoyed great popularity in dog training. When you go into pet shops perhaps you have already noticed a clicker among the dog accessories. It looks like a type of small box that works like a click frog. You press on it to make a clear clicking noise. You may wonder what's so special about this sound. At first, nothing, for only through appropriate training does it take on a special meaning. This type of training is not new. Perhaps you have even experienced it unknowingly, specifically in a zoo. Seals, whales, and even apes and other animals learn their tricks according to this principle. Dolphins and seals, for example, cannot be influenced through a leash or a rein; therefore, it is necessary to find other ways to show them what behavior we are looking for.

Clicker training became popular in the field of dog training especially through Karen Pryor, an American zoologist and dolphin trainer. But the real "inventor" of an important part of clicker training was the Russian doctor and Nobel-prize winner Ivan Petrovitch Pavlov (1849–1936). Over a certain period of time he connected the feeding of his laboratory dogs with a bell tone, and thus observed an interesting phenomenon: after a certain number of repetitions the dogs began to drool upon merely hearing the bell, as if they had their dish full of food before them.

Now you have a better understanding of what's behind clicker training. In the following pages you will find out precisely how it works.

How Clicker Training Works

To make the principle of clicker training easy to understand, we will now take a brief side trip into the realm of canine learning behavior.

Primary and Secondary Reinforcement

In order to encourage a behavior by your dog in a positive manner, you need reinforcement in the form of a reward (see page 7).

The more stimulating the reward is for the "pupil," the more effective it is. If a reinforcement is naturally of great significance, we speak of a primary reinforcement. With dogs an example of this is food. By nature it is extremely significant, even vitally important to them.

For a dog with the appropriate predisposition, this can also be a ball flying through the air. But the problem is that you cannot always give a dog a treat or throw a ball for it at the right instant in every situation in which you want to reward it. Imagine that you want to get the dog to pick up an object from the floor and the dog does so. Now when you reach into your pocket for a treat, the dog immediately drops the object and fixates only on the pocket where the treats are kept. In such situations the timing for the reward is optimized by what's known as a secondary reinforcement that instantly tells the dog, "Well done; now you will get a tasty treat."

Do you remember the Russian doctor Pavlov and his bell that I told you about on page 5? The sound of the bell, which initially was meaningless to the dog, practically turns into a type of food dish through the connection with the "natural" stimulation of food; it produces the same reaction, namely salivation, for the dog knows that "Soon I will get food."

In clicker training the clicker becomes the secondary positive reinforcement because it is connected momentarily with food.

This dog expectantly watches its owner for the click, promptly followed by a treat!

For further clarification let's return briefly to the dolphins. In this instance the secondary reinforcement is a certain whistle. It signals to the dolphin, for example, at the high point of a jump, that it was especially good. But only after performing the jump does the dolphin get its fish. To round things off let's take another look in our world, for here too there are primary and secondary reinforcements. Eating and drinking are examples of primary reinforcements for us. Money, on the other hand, is a secondary reinforcement. We have learned that we can buy food and drink with money; therefore we are happy when we get money, and exert ourselves to get it—otherwise, would you work? But there are also negative primary reinforcements. One example of this is pain (such as that caused by an electrical stimulus). Even this type of reinforcement can be associated with a neutral stimulus, such as turning on a lamp. The lamp then becomes a negative secondary reinforcement; it signifies pain and leads to a behavior that avoids the electrical stimulus, even though it is not turned on. An example of a secondary negative reinforcement in our environment is a roadside radar speed indicator. As soon as we see it, we automatically slow down to the speed limit. We have learned that there are negative consequences for us if we drive too fast when this type of device is at the side of the road.

Classic Conditioning The learning process in which the primary reinforcement is associated with the subsequent, secondary reinforcement is known as classic conditioning.

Positive and Negative Reinforcement

One further aspect of clicker training is the principle of positive reinforcement: a reward follows desired behavior. This works the same way with

1 Food is naturally of great importance to dogs. The dog does not first need to learn what it means; therefore food is a primary reinforcement.

2 Like food, play is naturally positive for dogs; therefore both things are positive primary reinforcements.

3 Only through association with food does the initially neutral sound of the clicker take on meaning; the clicker becomes a secondary reinforcement.

dogs as with humans. When a stimulating reward beckons, we are prepared to do something for it. Learning in this way is free of anxiety and negative stress. There is abundant positive stress.

In contrast to positive reinforcement, negative reinforcement is also used in dog training. With this the dog experiences a negative sensation, which it can terminate through desired behavior.

Let's look at an example to understand the difference. You want to teach your dog the new exercise *"Down!"* Through positive reinforcement using treats, the dog is motivated to lie down. It can get the morsel only by lying in the appropriate position. If the dog does not obey, there simply is no treat.

In training through negative reinforcement, the trainer steps on the leash so that the dog is pulled downward from a sitting or standing position. As soon as it lies down, the leash is slackened. You will not find it difficult to imagine which of these two scenarios the dog will learn more thoroughly and confidently.

Operant Conditioning The dog learns certain behaviors because it experiences success with them—there is a reward, or a negative sensation ceases. This is referred to as learning through operant conditioning.

Thus, the clicker, after first becoming a secondary reinforcement, is nothing more than the reward for desirable behavior on the part of the dog.

Positive and Negative Punishment

Dogs don't always do what they are supposed to do. In order for them to learn what you want and don't want, undesirable behavior must have consequences. In connection with training through

Clicker training makes it possible to reinforce many types of behavior. Real experts can perform their tricks enthusiastically even in the presence of major distractions.

positive reinforcement, including clicker training, negative punishment also comes into play. In this sense *negative* means that something pleasant is taken away or withheld.

Thus, if the dog learns something new and does not exhibit the desired behavior, such as *"Sit!,"* there is no click. Another example: the dog already knows how to sit but doesn't do it. You don't throw the beloved ball until the dog sits. There is no reward.

In order for this to work, the reward must be more important to the dog than anything else. And it must not have any alternatives it considers worthwhile, such as digging for a mouse. That's the only way the dog will be motivated to eventually show the desired behavior.

As a counterpoint to this there is positive punishment: an unpleasant stimulus is introduced. For example, the dog is pulling on the leash and is reprimanded with a pull on the leash.

But one risk with positive punishment is not finding the right dose. If it is too strong, or if the dog really does not understand that it is supposed to walk on a slack leash, for example, it can cause the dog to lose trust in its human and lead to major

uncertainty. Thus, learning through positive punishment is counterproductive, especially in combination with clicker training, since it additionally restricts the dog's motivation.

In order to manage in such situations, you need a negative command. When a dog securely masters a signal, it must comply. This is particularly crucial in basic obedience, not for tricks. You can work effectively with body language and voice to carry this through, but depending on the type of dog, a negative reinforcement may also be necessary (also see pages 52–59).

Learning through positive motivation is easier and more desirable than training with punishments.

Preparations for Clicker Training

Focused

DISTRACTION-FREE AREA
In order for you and your dog to concentrate most effectively on the clicking, at the start of every exercise you need an environment free of distractions. Distraction may mean something different to the dog than to you, though, for even the favorite ball in a corner of the room may act as an excessive, irresistible stimulus.

Timing

CLICKING AT PRECISELY THE RIGHT INSTANT This is done at the right moment. This is the only time when your dog can understand which behavior was correct. If the click comes at the wrong instant, it sends the dog down the wrong path. So observe your dog carefully so that you can click on small actions in the right direction. During an exercise, always keep the clicker in your hand so you can react quickly enough when necessary. Success will soon follow.

Shhh!

QUIET While the dog is discovering what the clicker means, don't speak to it, as that disturbs the learning process. You can combine a brief verbal reward with the treat only after the click.

Treat

QUICK REWARD In order for your dog to connect the click and the treat directly and most effectively, at least in the conditioning phase, the treat should be small and relatively soft. That allows the dog to swallow the reward quickly and easily. If it has to chew a piece of food for a longer time, and crumbs fall onto the floor, the dog is quickly distracted and the important correlation is disrupted.

Distracting

STEP BY STEP Only when an exercise is truly under control should the dog perform it under distraction. Don't increase the external stimulus until the previous exercise is mastered perfectly.

The Advantages of Clicker Training

You now know what the clicker is: a secondary reinforcement that is used in training by way of positive
reinforcement. But what is the advantage of the
clicker? How do you condition the dog to the
clicker? How do you approach an exercise? There
are a few things to keep in mind concerning these
questions. The clicker is no magical cure, but it has
a few advantages in comparison to training without
a clicker, especially for learning tricks and stunts.

A Unique Sound   Couldn't you use a specific
word instead? Yes, in theory the food could be
linked to *"Good,"* and this word would then
become the secondary reinforcement. Most dog
owners even do this more or less unconsciously,
but not really precisely.

The disadvantage is that the dog hears your
voice and that of the other family members all day
long. In addition, many people talk too much and

You wish to reward the dog for looking at the ball. The clicker has no peer for confirmation
at the best possible instant. The timing is exactly right.

too randomly with their dogs, so that the voice loses effectiveness for the dog. Can you also be sure that the dog is hearing the command exclusively in connection with the training? That could be difficult.

On the other hand, the clicker is a unique and noticeable sound in the dog's everyday life. It is simple to use, and unlike words it is not used by chance.

The clicker must always be stored securely so that your children don't take it for an amusing click frog and play with it. In that case the clicker would lose its meaning.

Long-distance Reward   Even when your dog is not right by your side you can reward it at the right instant with the clicker. If you want to teach your dog to roll a ball, it can be a fair distance away. The reward consists of a click, for *click* means *"Well done, here comes a treat!"*

Precise Timing   The clicker makes it possible to reinforce the dog at precisely the right moment. It doesn't matter if it's a specific movement or posture. With a little practice you will easily recognize the right instant.

Facilitating Communication   Basic obedience exercises don't necessarily require a clicker, but rather the deliberate use of voice and body language. Many dog owners find it difficult to change the pitch of their voices or to communicate properly with their dogs through body language. The clicker facilitates communication.

Voraciousness   If a dog is very voracious, or if the association with treats and rewards is instilled incorrectly, it often is so fixated on the treat pocket or your hand that it can't concentrate on anything else. This is remedied with the clicker.

A **Variety of Rewards**

TIPS FROM THE
CLICKER EXPERT

DON'T JUST CLICK   Do you always have to confirm your dog with the clicker? That is not necessary and even would be somewhat inconvenient, for you would always have to have the clicker with you.

PRAISING AND PETTING   As skill increases you can praise your dog in different ways and for special accomplishments, including with the clicker. When the dog can do the exercise perfectly and reliably on signal, the voice, petting, or a little play are adequate rewards.

CUTTING BACK ON THE CLICKER   With an exercise that the dog has mastered you can gradually cut back on the clicker and do without it. In principle the dog must be amply reinforced for an accomplished performance. If this confirmation is lacking, over the long run the performance will become sloppy or fall by the wayside altogether.

INDIVIDUAL DIFFERENCES   With tractable, motivated dogs you usually can cut back on rewards and confirmations; however, dogs that are apathetic or easily distracted need significantly more help with motivation.

What's Involved in Clicker Training

The Right Reward

Dogs are willing to demonstrate behaviors that are somehow worthwhile to them. In order for the dog to be as highly motivated as possible, the clicker must promise an extraordinarily appealing reward. That is the only way it can function as an effective secondary reinforcement. But what is "appealing" can vary considerably from dog to dog. Whereas regular dry food nuggets may be true highlights for one dog, another finds them boring but is prepared to do anything for a little piece of cheese.

Before working with a dog, you should find out what it considers the ultimate reward. At the beginning, food makes the most sense; it is simple and practical and can be used in all situations. In addition, after receiving the reward, the dog is with you and under control. For most dogs food is the effective primary reinforcement. Once the learning is solidified and the dog is "into" other things, then the reward can occasionally take a different form. Thus, tossing a ball can be an attractive reward after the click. If the dog likes to romp with other dogs, the exuberant play can be a reward, for example, after the dog has maintained eye contact

Every exercise is practiced without distraction until the dog spontaneously offers the behavior.

Once the dog displays the behavior spontaneously for some time, the distraction can increase, and the surroundings can change.

with you for a fairly long time, even though the other dogs are within the field of view.

No matter what you offer your dog as a reward after the click, it must be something it really likes. Here's another thing to consider: in working with food, your dog should always be a little hungry. Subtract the treats from its daily ration, and always work with the dog before feeding, never right afterward.

Conditioning the Dog to the Clicker

Before getting started, the program includes conditioning to the clicker; only when the dog has learned the meaning of the clicker can the desired effect be produced. First get everything ready. You need a quiet, familiar environment, preferably inside the house. You also need a portion of small, fairly soft treats that the dog can swallow without chewing, or the temporal correlation between the click and swallowing the reward becomes too long.

You can either place the treats on a table or keep them in your pocket. In any case you must be able to grab them quickly. Hold the clicker in the other hand. The hungry dog is in the immediate vicinity. You may even hold it on a leash. Then here goes! Click and immediately give the dog a treat. Then click again, and promptly give the dog another treat. Repeat this about ten to fifteen times over the period of just a few minutes, then take a break so it doesn't become boring.

If, for example, the first training session took place in the morning, repeat the entire exercise in the afternoon. Usually that is adequate, and the dog understands that the click announces a treat. You can test this by clicking while the dog is looking the other way. If the dog looks at you expec-

Only when an exercise works properly in various places and under distraction should you introduce the accompanying signal.

tantly, it understands what is going on. You will quickly notice that your dog is on task, attentive and motivated, as soon as you take out the clicker.

Things to Look Out For

> Be sure to give the dog a treat after every click, so there is no click without a treat. Always click before you give the treat, not after.

> In the second training session gradually stretch out the time between the click and the treat to several seconds. Because, as already mentioned, with many exercises the dog is not right by your side, but will be rewarded by the click. The treat is then delayed for a moment.

> Don't reach for the treat right before clicking, but only after. Otherwise, you are conditioning the dog to your hand movement in the direction of the treats. This must be avoided.

› In the course of the second training session you can put the treats further away. For example, you can stand in the center of the room, with the treats several feet away on a table. The dog must concentrate on you, not on the treats.

› It is irrelevant whether the dog is sitting, lying down, or standing when you condition it to the clicker. It is even advantageous if it is not always in the same position, or this will also become conditioned. The dog should merely connect "Click—a treat," so you should also change your position so that the dog does not connect the exercise with a particular position. For example, during the training

session occasionally go to a different corner of the room or even into a different room.

› If you suspect that the clicker sound may be too loud for your dog, mute it somewhat. For example, activate the clicker behind your back or inside the pocket of your pants or jacket. If the dog remains relaxed, gradually click without the muting.

The Structure of an Exercise

Dog training must be systematic, whether with or without a clicker. A systematic structure makes it easier for the dog to understand what you want from it, and protects it from overload. In addition, the learning is reliably solidified at every degree of difficulty.

Proceeding too quickly easily makes the dog feel insecure, and the learning doesn't really take hold. Following training, ultimately the goal is for your dog to perform the exercise when you wish and you give it the appropriate signal (command). Before you begin with a specific exercise, you must have the dog conditioned to the clicker as described on page 15.

Breaking Down the Exercise A complex exercise is first broken down into individual steps and built up in stages. As an example, let's take touching the nose to a wand stuck into the ground some distance away from you.

› Begin by simply having the dog nudge the wand as you hold it in your hand.

› Change the location of the wand slightly so that the dog must go to it intentionally.

› Now the distance is increased.

Let the conditioning begin! Now activate the clicker for the first time.

Don't reach for a treat until just after clicking. This is extremely important for establishing the most effective correlation.

Now give the dog the luscious treat. The next "click–treat sequence" begins only after the dog has finished eating the treat.

Since such complex exercises are not easy to begin with, at first it is better to choose something easier, such as touching the tip of the rod or making eye contact with you. The fewer the individual steps, the clearer the exercise is for both you and the dog.

Waiting Once you have decided on an exercise, it now comes down to the dog's showing of its own accord the desired behavior or an attempt at it. To the extent possible it should figure out what it is supposed to do in order to hear the promising click.

You have already prepared treats and are holding the clicker in your hand. Your dog will presumably come to you expectantly and try various things. It may nudge you, invite you to play, or lie down. You simply do nothing. Sticking with the eye-contact example, whenever the dog looks at you briefly, click, and the dog gets a treat.

Many dogs look like things are rattling around in their head as they try to figure out why they got the reward. For you this merely involves waiting a little

longer and observing. Once your dog shows the behavior again, click and treat.

The Right Reward In order for your dog to figure out what it is supposed to do, every time your dog does the right thing, give a click. This changes once you notice that your dog displays the behavior on its own in order to get a reward—but not until then.

Timely Help

SUSTAINING INTEREST In clicker training the dog normally should find out all by itself which behavior generates the click. But an inexperienced beginner dog should not attempt without success for too long, or it may give up. So help it at the beginning if you sense that its interest might flag.

Now not every correct behavior gets a click, but only now and again, on a variable basis, sometimes on the second time, sometimes even later, and occasionally even after one time. Not too infrequently, though, for otherwise the dog will lose interest. Even if there is a treat every time, the interest can decline over time. If the dog does something particularly well, after the click there is a "jackpot"—a handful of treats or something totally special. Rewarding on a variable basis has the effect of keeping the dog's expectant behavior high. This is similar to a slot machine. People keep playing because they could win at any time.

Increasing the Demands   Once the exercise works reliably and the dog participates happily, increase the demands. For example, give the dog its click when it looks at you for a longer time. Also change the surroundings so that your dog does not connect the exercise with a special environment.

Introducing Signals   Has it occurred to you that so far we have not talked about any signals? At first the dog figured out for itself what it has to do in order to get a reward. In the meantime it displays the desired behavior reliably and at a high level, that is, even with distractions and in different surroundings, or precisely the way you have imagined the end result. The dog still performs it purely on its own, in order to get a reward. Now is the time to introduce an auditory or a visual signal, for ultimately this is the way you want to see and call up the exercise. For example, after practicing, when the dog touches the rod or looks at you in the eye-contact exercise, you give your command at the same time, that is, as soon as the dog begins to do it (*"Look"* in the eye-contact example). Don't speak the command much in advance, for the dog does not yet know what it means. But if it hears the command just as it begins the exercise, it can make the connection. Give the command only, once that happens after several repetitions, and your dog will henceforth show the trained behavior.

For many dogs a particular game is a more stimulating reward than a treat.

Targeted Demands Now comes the last step. The dog gets confirmation only when it displays the behavior upon your demand. It probably will still do it on its own in order to get a reward, but now it gets nothing more for it. Keep practicing under a wide variety of conditions so that the exercise works everywhere. You must be able to call up the material learned in every situation. A reward is given only when the exercise is done particularly well—for example, with the eye contact exercise, when the dog looks at you immediately and for a long time; but the dog will come up empty-handed with a sloppy or a delayed performance.

A Few More Rules

> Be patient. Ideally the dog should figure out on its own what you want from it. Help it only if necessary, and as little as possible. Again, take eye contact as an example. If the dog does not look at you even after a fairly long time, then use the clicker just at the beginning. But eventually do away with such aids.

> Always click just one time per desired behavior, not more.

> If you increase the demands, do so only when the exercise works with absolute reliability on the previous level.

> Depending on the exercise and the type of dog, it is important to click the instant the dog starts to display the desired behavior. Let's consider the example of sitting. One dog is willing to sit on its own and quickly. It is adequate for you to click as soon as it sits.

Another dog merely lowers its bottom a bit, but stands up immediately to do something else or to try a different behavior. In this case you should click while the hindquarters are moving downward.

Learning Trust in Small Steps

Dogs that have had bad experiences with humans are often fearful and refuse or resist being touched. Clicker training can also help in this situation.

ACTION	HOW TO DO IT
NO PHYSICAL CONTACT	The dog refuses to be touched or influenced in any way by a leash. If it will not take treats from the hand at first, toss them onto the floor. Try to build up trust with very simple exercises. That way the dog will learn that it can be very pleasant to have contact with a human.
THE FIRST TOUCH	The training without physical contact may give the dog enough confidence to spontaneously establish contact, for example by putting a paw onto your foot or nudging you gently. This always gets a click. Perhaps the dog will also put up with a touch from you—click. Try to slowly prolong the contact.
DON'T PRACTICE ALONE	With difficulties of this type it is crucial to gauge the dog correctly. You should therefore get help from a competent trainer with experience in dealing with problem dogs.

If you avoid reinforcing the rudimentary sitting, eventually the dog will cease to display that behavior. Ultimately it is not worth it to the dog.

> Do not scold the dog if it fails to display precisely the desired behavior, or if in working on a new exercise it first "performs" something it can already do, especially when the dog is trying to figure out how it can earn the reward. That would inhibit it and reduce its individual initiative.

If the dog does not display the correct behavior, but rather some other exercise, for example, then you can connect withholding the reward with *"Wrong!"* (see page 34). But don't use the word that indicates to the dog that something is completely taboo—thus, don't use the word you would use when your dog is chewing an electrical cord or starting to roll in some filth, for example.

Every **Click** Is Followed by a **Treat**

ONE CLICK Click just once for a desired behavior, not several times in succession.

ALWAYS REWARD After every click there is a treat; this also includes when you click accidentally.

LOSS OF MOTIVATION If there is repeatedly no treat, the clicker quickly becomes meaningless.

> Plan small training units to keep your dog from becoming overwhelmed or losing interest. If you practice several units, one after another, insert a break between them. Play with your dog or let it run.

> In order for the dog to know when the instruction is beginning and ending, connect the start and the end with an extra signal, such as *"Clicker!"* and *"All done!"*

> To keep your dog from becoming conditioned to a specific "treat hand," keep changing hands. That way it sometimes gets a treat from the right hand, and sometimes from the left.

> Be sure to click at the instant when the dog demonstrates the desired behavior, not after.

> The click announces the treat and simultaneously ends the behavior just performed. It does not need to be terminated verbally as well.

If you are patient and follow a few basic rules, you can train your dog to obey you. However, if you experience problems training your dog, a professional trainer should be called in for assistance.

PLAY If a game has a high value for the dog, then also combine it with a click as a reward, preferably at the end of an exercise. Throw the dog's favorite ball when it brings it back to you. Or play a game of tug, but always with rules. Usually you are the winner, and you determine the start and the end of the game. A short game is adequate as a reward. Always stop before the dog loses interest.

FOOD With most creatures food is a high priority and is thus very appropriate to associate with the clicker, especially for the initial conditioning. In contrast to playing, it does not take the dog entirely out of the situation, and when done properly, it does not interrupt the concentration; therefore it is particularly appropriate as a reward even for rudimentary correct behavior and intermediate steps.

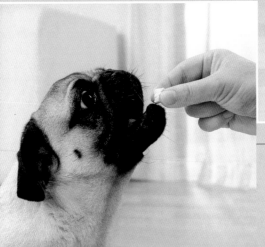

UNIQUE In order for the clicker to announce something really good, the treats must be stimulating to the dog, preferably small and relatively soft. Tastes certainly can vary.

The First Practical Exercise Without the Dog

We are done with the theory! Now the practice begins, but first without the dog. This way it is easier for you to try out and practice the use of the clicker. In addition, these dry runs are a lot of fun. You will need one more person, and of course, a clicker.

One Person Plays "Dog"

In this dry run in the house, one person takes on the role of the dog and is sent out of the room. The other person plays the role of the dog owner, holds the clicker, and plans an exercise that the "dog" must perform, for example, going to a specific chair and placing the hand (paw) on the backrest.

The exercise quickly becomes fun when you give a click for every movement and action in the proper direction!

The Individual Steps

As already mentioned, complex tasks are first broken down into steps. In our exercise the "dog" must first move around the room, go in the right direction, do something with the left hand (paw), and finally place it on the backrest—not such a simple task. Once the task is clear, the "dog" is brought into the room. Now it must attempt to discover what its task is. The "dog" may skip over individual steps, or it may take longer. Of course this applies not only to the two-legged "dog," but also to training with the real one.

Reinforcing the Right Steps

The other person observes the "dog" closely. Let's assume that the "dog" moves around the room. There is always a click every time it moves in the direction of the right chair. There is an additional click for every further movement in the proper direction. Once the "dog" arrives at the chair, it must figure out what it is supposed to do. It will attempt various things. Once again every action in the right direction is reinforced, for example, when it moves the left hand (paw). In theory it could also happen that it goes away from the chair, then every new action in the direction of the chair is once again reinforced with the clicker. The more precise the clicking, the quicker the "dog" will discover just what it is to do. It will be happy at every click, because it has done something correctly.

"Punishment" Inhibits

Envision the whole exercise in the following way. If the two-legged "dog" is always scolded with a strict

"No!" every time it does something wrong, such as remaining standing, going in the wrong direction, moving the wrong paw, and so forth, it will hardly have the confidence to try anything, since it keeps experiencing failure, so it decides to do nothing, rather than something wrong.

Things could be different with a friendly vocal signal such as *"Cold!"* In a new exercise if the "dog" tries to do the same as before, *"Cold!"* communicates that this is the wrong direction, but it can make headway by trial and error. That motivates it. Provided, of course, that the test person knows precisely how the principle of clicker training works and what the correction word *"Cold"* entails (see Expert Advice, page 34).

If you enjoy this game then swap roles and think of other tasks to perform.

Pay close attention! Can you click the instant the ball touches the floor? It's not so easy to do.

Exercises with a Ball

The right timing is a crucial factor with clicking. It is even said that you can't make any mistakes in clicking that lead to negative consequences, in contrast to training through force and similar means, for example. But that's not entirely true; depending on the situation, a click at the wrong instant can reinforce an undesired or even problematical behavior. So in dog training in general, and in clicker training, make sure that you reward at the proper time.

You can practice the precise timing with these two exercises:

› Your helper drops a ball—preferably on a hard surface so that the ball bounces. Try to click at the precise instant the ball hits the floor for the first time.

› This variation is a little more difficult: The helper tosses a ball up and you try to click when the ball reaches its highest point, but not when it is already on the "return." Can you do it? Here the advantage of the clicker once again becomes clear. In similar situations in training with the dog you simply cannot reward it without a secondary reinforcement. And you can imagine that this training is totally indispensable with creatures such as whales and seals.

The Clicker in Everyday Practice

The theory and dry runs are now behind you, and you have gained a feel for this training method. Your dog is conditioned to the clicker and looks on expectantly when you pick up the clicker. Now it is time to put it into practice with the dog!

The Most Important Exercises for Every Day

All basic obedience exercises are perfect for training with the clicker. Just always keep in mind the sequential structure (see pages 16–17):

› Wait for the desired behavior in surroundings with the least possible distractions.

› Click as soon as the dog displays or comes close to the behavior pattern.

› Keep clicking over the course of several training sessions, but then gradually use the clicker variably and for particularly good performances.

› Increase the demands successively and train in different, less familiar, or unknown surroundings.

› Introduce a signal.

› In the final step, reward the four-legged pupil only when it carries out the task upon your command—and even here you should click variably.

When your dog knows and masters the eight most important obedience exercises, it will experience no problems and misunderstandings in daily life.

Every exercise should be trained carefully. Patience and regular repetition are the guarantees for successful and stable training.

"Look!"

The goal of this exercise is the eye contact that the dog makes with you upon your signal. Eye contact is the essential prerequisite for almost every interaction with the dog, to the extent that this unit is almost the basic exercise of basic exercises and the ideal starting point.

Later on, eye contact should be made in the presence of distractions; for example, in the presence of other dogs or of joggers. With this it is not crucial whether your dog is sitting, standing, or lying down.

How It Works Maybe your dog already looks expectantly when it sees the clicker in your hand; then it's time for a click and a reward. If the dog immediately makes eye contact again after eating the treat, follow up with another click and a treat. Otherwise, wait for it to look at you. At first, distraction is taboo: practice in surroundings with little distraction so that the dog cannot find a more interesting alternative. Once it understands the connection, acknowledge the increasingly long eye contact. Training will then continue with distractions, and the signal will be added.

Possible Help If your dog doesn't look at you at all, at first click your tongue—but only until making the first eye contact.

Grooming on a Click

GROOMING GROUCHES Does your dog not like it when you check its teeth, ears, and eyes? Practice the chores with the clicker.

TOUCHING PERMITTED The ears, for example: Click when your dog tolerates a brief touch on the ears. Gradually increase the contact and ultimately wipe out the ears.

CLICK FOR THE EARDROPS Grasp the ear and hold the bottle with the ear cleaner over it—click! Keep bringing the bottle closer to the ear, until the first drop finally lands in the ear. Proceed similarly for other types of care.

HELP Since both hands are needed for many types of care, a second person should take over the clicker.

"Come!"

Your dog must immediately come to you without any detours, even from fairly far away and in the presence of distractions.

How It Works The dog is separated from you by a short distance. Draw its attention to you either by calling it (saying its name), or commanding *"Look!"* Increase the distance by walking backward quickly as soon as the dog makes eye contact. Click when it comes to you and reward it with a little treat or a game.

The quicker it comes, the more stimulating the reward should be. If the dog reacts happily and is visibly motivated, then use the signal while it is running to you. That can be *"Come!"* but a tweet with the dog whistle is even more striking.

Increase the distraction and the distance slowly so that the dog internalizes the procedure. For the first week or two, practice only indoors. Thereafter, the training can be moved outside, preferably in the yard at first.

Possible Help You will have to lend a hand with a somewhat inattentive dog. A helper can hold onto it by the collar or by the chest. Show the dog a treat and run away with it. The dog will want to chase you. As soon as you are a little further away, the helper releases the dog. Turn toward it and click while it is running to you. Once it reaches you, of course it gets the treat.

Extra Tip Help from a second person also makes sense when the dog is expected to come to you as you whistle from quite far away. It sees you get further away but cannot chase you because it is being held. In this situation the "releasing" whistle is the highlight and becomes effectively imprinted.

You are ready; the clicker is in your hand, and the treats are where you can reach them. But the dog still is not making eye contact with you.

Here's where we are: the dog is looking at you—click and treat. Initially always click at the precise instant its gaze meets yours.

"Sit!"

Sitting is one of the simplest exercises. The goal is for the dog to sit down immediately and calmly remain seated near you for a couple of minutes.

How It Works You have already half-won if your dog sits willingly and full of expectation as soon as it sees the clicker in your hand. Now simply click and reward the dog. It's best to toss the treat a few feet away onto the ground so that the dog has to stand up. Then it can sit again. If your dog appears a bit hesitant, click every time as soon as it even shows a tendency to sit, such as when its bottom moves in a downward direction. With each click it will move lower still. Reinforce even the smallest progress. Once the dog sits willingly, first increase the duration, and then the distraction. The vocal command is *"Sit!"* and the raised hand can also serve as a visual cue.

Possible Help If the dog does not sit, a treat will entice it. Hold the treat just above its head and ignore it if it barks, stands up, or jumps for the treat. The hand remains in the same position and is closed only to keep the dog from getting the treat. Eventually it will sit; then it gets a click and the treat.

"Down!"

Lying down and remaining in that position for a fairly long time and under distraction has many advantages in the daily dealings with the dog—for example, in visiting an outdoor restaurant, where your four-legged companion can lie comfortably and relaxed under the table.

How It Works For the first training unit, choose a time after a long walk or a wild session of sports and games. The dog is worn out and tired and is happy to lie down. Go into a quiet room with it and wait for it to lie down on its own—click and treat. With this exercise also, throw the treat a distance away to prompt the dog to stand up. After that, if the dog lies down again, proceed as always—click and treat. As soon as the dog reliably demonstrates the desired behavior, the time leading up to the click is gradually lengthened so that the dog remains in place longer. Then, once again, increase the distraction, change the training location, and introduce the signal. *"Down!"* works well in combination with a downward hand movement.

Possible Help Does your bundle of energy never get really tired? Or does it take forever for it to lie down? Then use a treat as an aid. If your dog spontaneously sits next to you, hold the treat in front of its nose and move it slowly straight down, not forward; in that case the dog will stand up, that way it will follow the treat with its eyes and automatically lie down—click and reward.

Extra Tip Hold the hand with the treat under a low table or your bended leg. The only way the dog can get the treat is to lie down.

"Stay!"

At the start of this exercise the dog should already know how to sit or lie calmly next to you (see page 27). Now you can get it used to remaining in this position even when you go away from it. The goal of the exercise: remaining in place until your return. The dog should wait calmly for you; therefore it is more comfortable for a fairly long time if the dog is lying down. Once the *stay* is working well you can call the dog out of the *sit* and to you. Never call the dog out of the *down* position, for later on it must remain lying calmly even under distraction or when you are out of its field of view.

How It Works Have the dog lie down beside you. Place yourself about 8 inches (20 cm) in front of it and then return to its side—click. At first increase only the length of time, and save the distance for later. Once you can go some distance

away from the dog for two to three minutes, you can walk back and forth parallel to the dog in a gradually increasing radius. One day you can hide behind a tree or a bush, for just a moment at first, and then for longer. The command *"Stay!"* is given immediately before you go away. Visual cue: hold the palm of the hand a short distance in front of the dog's face. In practicing with a sitting dog, the duration and distance are kept short.

Possible Help Does your dog not get it? Then you can tie it to a tree with a leash or have a helper hold it. Now it cannot follow you. Depending on the exercise, click as soon as it lies down or sits.

"Stand!"

Having the dog stand calmly has applications beyond the leash and the veterinarian's office.

How It Works Perhaps there is already a situation in which the dog remains standing calmly for a brief time. Click and reward! When it sits or lies down, back up a few steps to motivate it to stand up, but not to chase you. Again, click and reward. Later on, reinforce standing for a longer time under

---

Click Only for **Specific Exercises**

TREATS FOR OBEDIENCE Do you prefer to practice basic obedience with your dog with treats and without a clicker, or has your dog already learned the exercises without treats? That's all fine. But you can still condition it to the clicker and use the click only for tricks or complex exercises.

REWARDING THE STARTING POINT This dog has already tried several things, but nothing in the direction of sitting. Now its hind end drops slightly. This is the right moment for the click. The dog will soon figure out what you want but if there is no click, there is a reduced probability for a renewed approach in the right direction. Observe your dog carefully so you can click at the best possible time.

TIMING The dog should maintain eye contact. It looks attentively at its mistress. Since this moment can be rather brief, you need to watch carefully and react in a timely fashion. Even a slight hesitation is enough to reinforce looking away—that is, the opposite of what you want. But if the click comes at the right instant, the dog will hold eye contact longer in anticipation of the click.

MISSION ACCOMPLISHED This is what perfect heeling looks like. The dog remains close to the side of its human and shows full attention. This is worth a click and the jackpot!

distraction and in unfamiliar surroundings. Also practice so that your dog accepts being touched all over.

Possible Help Is this exercise too difficult for your dog? If it continues sitting down, or you cannot seize the right moment because the dog is too lively, use a treat as an aid. Move it forward horizontally so that the dog stands up. Once it stands up, hold your hand still—click.

Careful: don't hold the treat up high, or the dog will sit down. In order to further reinforce the standing, you may also place your hand under the dog's belly.

"Heel!"

The dog should walk right next to you on a slack leash, on either the right or the left. It is desirable for it to maintain eye contact.

How It Works This is practiced on a loose leash or without a leash. *"Look"* (see pages 25–26) is an ideal warm-up, of course with a reward. Then take off quickly, perhaps with a short alluring run. If the dog follows you, click and reward, even while it is still moving. Take off again but this time don't click until it gets closer to you, and right after it catches up to you.

At first it is okay if the dog stays with you for only a couple of strides. Gradually increase the distance. This works best at a brisk pace. Later on, see if your dog remains at your side through an undulating course and a figure-eight. Now introduce the command *"Heel!"*

Practice this on varied terrain and with obstacles such as stumps or stairs, and with distractions (cyclists, joggers). Your dog is the perfect companion when it keeps looking at you.

Possible Help Hold a treat in your left hand while the dog walks at your left side. Your arm hangs down straight, and while you walk, the dog can lap the treat and thus stay in the desired position—a click and a reward follow.

Little by little the treat and the hand move into the jacket pocket. The dog goes along, looks at you, and feels validated.

Walking calmly on a slack leash is rewarded with a click. Impatient pulling is not.

"Slowly!"

Even when the dog is on a leash, it need not always walk right by your feet. But of course it also must not pull on the leash. A dog on a loose leash makes every walk twice as much fun.

How It Works Click and reward the dog when it happens to go along on a slack leash for a short distance. If it pulls on the leash, stop until the leash is no longer taut. Signal the imminent forced break to your dog with a warning of *"No!"* or *"Stop!"* The dog must never experience success or get its way by tugging on the leash.

Connect walking on a loose leash with a calm command of *"Slowly!"* and gradually increase the duration and the distraction. If your dog wants to sniff something where another dog has marked, it must not pull you to the spot. But if the leash remains loose, a click follows, and instead of a treat the dog gets to sniff.

The strategy also applies when the dog wants to greet acquaintances you meet on a walk. Reward the dog variably, by sometimes letting it go where it wants, and not at other times, in spite of a loose leash. Just continue walking.

Possible Help Training is particularly easy when your dog is tuckered out and you practice in distraction-free surroundings.

The **Right Signals**

TIPS FROM THE
CLICKER EXPERT

EXPLICIT AND CLEAR Choose the signals carefully. Use explicit words and gestures that are clearly different from one another and that you use in no other context.

THE TONE OF VOICE COUNTS The terms should not be used too commonly in daily conversation or there is a danger that the dog will not be able to relate to them. Pay attention to the right tone of voice so the commands are distinguishable from the intonation of normal conversation.

DON'T ASK TOO MUCH Don't begin several new exercises at once. That can confuse the dog, since it will be rewarded for a variety of behaviors.

TRAINING TIME Exercises and tricks you have already been working on for some time are best practiced separated from one another temporarily, for example at different times of the day. This is particularly true for exercises that are similar to one another in structure and demands. Of course you can call up tasks that the dog does well at any time and any place.

Exercises with a Target Wand

Dogs enjoy learning and like to be kept busy. Clicker training offers plenty of possibilities for this. Here you will find a selection of ideas, but surely you have others. Here too, always consider the proper structure for the exercise (see pages 16–17). Also be considerate of your dog and don't require anything of it that is too taxing physically or mentally.

"Touch!"

For this exercise you simply need something like a rod. One good possibility is a telescoping target wand, which you can buy in pet shops and online. The dog learns to touch the end of the wand. The touch exercise is an ideal entry into clicker training and will prove very useful later on with various other tricks and exercises.

This dog knows *"Touch!"* With its nose on the tip of the target wand it is easy to lead it through the legs and reward it with a click.

How It Works Hold the tip of the wand in front of the dog's face. Wait until the dog happens to touch it with its nose or intentionally sniffs it. You can also arouse its interest by slightly moving the tip back and forth but you should not actively touch the dog's nose. When your dog nudges the tip of the wand, a click and reinforcement through a treat follow. Usually it won't take long for your dog to nudge the tip intentionally. Now begin to hold the wand in various positions, at first in front and to the side of your body at the height of the dog's nose so that the dog has to take a couple of steps to the wand.

Since the telescoping target wand can be extended, it is very easy to vary the distance a little. When the dog reliably and intentionally goes to the wand—whether you hold it to the right or the left, in front or behind—then you can hold the target tip even lower.

Depending on the dog's size, it may sometimes even have to lie down to touch the tip. Also try to hold the wand high enough so that your dog must stand on its hind legs to reach the tip. As with other exercises, change the surroundings after a while and introduce the command *"Touch!"* Then there is always a click whenever the dog touches the wand. After the click your dog will come back to get its reward.

Possible Help If the dog shows little or no interest in the wand, take a piece of hot dog in your hand and then rub your hand on the tip of the wand, or spread a little meat paste on it.

Variation Click when your dog keeps its nose on the tip of the wand for a longer time. Touching

Click when the dog touches the tip of the wand. After it learns this you can change the position of the wand in your hand.

Once the dog follows the wand in every position with its nose, place the tip on the ground a short distance away. Click when the dog touches it.

the wand for a longer time facilitates such things as keeping a small dog in the right position for heeling. Rambunctious and cautious dogs can both be led over various obstacles in this way. On a walk this can be a balancing exercise across a fallen tree trunk, and in dog sports, conquering the inclined wall.

Running Through Your Legs

The target wand is also the ideal aid for teaching a dog how to run through a person's legs and describe a figure-eight.

How It Works Move the wand in a figure-eight around your legs. The dog will follow the wand; then give a click when the figure-eight is complete. Once your dog understands the exercise, use a click only after the second figure-eight or even later.

Possible Help If the figure-eight is too difficult at first, have the dog run in a circle around one leg. Once that falls into place, add the run around the second leg.

Variation Have your dog run a slalom course through your legs. Take a fairly large step forward and direct the dog between your legs with the target wand. Then comes the next stride, and once again the dog is channeled around the leg and

How **Often to Click** in Training?

INCREMENTALLY The smaller the steps in the exercise, the better the dog will understand what it is supposed to do.

. . . AND CLICK Depending on the exercise, between 10 and 15 clicks per minute may be right.

INTENSIVE TRAINING Practice for a maximum of two minutes at a time, but several times a day. Pay attention to the dog's power of concentration.

Using a **Corrective Word**

TIPS FROM THE
CLICKER EXPERT

TONE OF VOICE The kindly spoken corrective word tells the dog that its behavior is not desirable, but that it should continue trying, and there is a reward at the end. It is not a prohibition.

USAGE Use the word only when the dog has some experience in clicker training and is not too sensitive—for example, when it is doing a familiar exercise, but you want to see something new.

MAKING THE CONNECTION Here's how it works: The dog brings two items in succession when they are lying on the floor apart from one another, and the dog is always rewarded with a click. When you put them both back down at the same time, the dog will be reinforced for the one it brings first. If the dog tries it again, you can say something like *"Too bad!"* If the dog picks up the other one after further unsuccessful attempts, give it a click. Reinforce this a couple of times. If the dog brings the other item again, repeat *"Too bad."*

ALTERNATIVE You have treats in each hand, and the dog heads for the hand it always gets treats from. Say *"Too bad."* When the dog goes to the other hand, it then gets a treat.

through the legs. Keep taking long strides while the dog runs a slalom around your legs.

"Go!"

Do you want your dog to go in a specific direction? As soon as it masters the *"Touch!"* exercise you can begin.

How It Works Stick the target wand into the ground—at the start of the exercise only 3 to 6 feet (1–2 m) away, but further away later on. Use your outstretched arm to show your dog the desired direction so it can get used to this signal from the beginning. Use the commands *"Forward!"* or *"Go!"* Set up the course to the wand with a little variety, for example, so that the dog has to jump over a log or ford a small brook. The path to the goal can also lead through a hedge or shrubbery. Always click when the dog touches the wand.

Variation Once your dog understands the hand signals indicating directions, you can work with several similar targets at the same time. Set out two target wands separated by 180 degrees and send the dog first to one and then to the other. The smaller the angle, the more demanding this exercise is for the dog.

› To send the dog right or left, have it sit facing you at the start of the exercise. The target wand is even with the dog and stuck in the ground to the right or the left of it. Now hold your right or left arm horizontal out to the side and send your pupil to the wand. A good vocal command is *"Away you go!"* You can of course also use *"Right!"* and *"Left!"* Gradually increase the distance between you and the dog and the distance between the dog and the wand.

› Once the dog masters each side individually, stick a target wand into the ground, both right and left, and send the dog to the one that was set up first.

› When the dog reaches the wand, give the commands *"Sit!"* or *"Down!"* That way you can have your dog lie down even at a distance. This exercise is part of many dog tests.

Extra Tip As soon as your dog masters the variations after a little training time and runs without hesitation in the direction you indicate and sits or lies down at a distance, put the wand away.

For dogs that like to fetch, you can now put out one or more items for fetching in place of the wand; then, you no longer use *"Sit!"* or *"Down!"*

Rolling a Ball

All ball games are super fun for dogs, and they provide lots of variety in the life of a dog. For training you need a large ball that your dog cannot pick up in its mouth.

This exercise assumes that your dog has already mastered the basic training for *"Touch!"* (see pages 32–33).

How It Works Move the ball with the tip of the target wand. Your dog will nudge it and simultaneously set the ball in motion.

Every time, click precisely when the ball starts to move even a bit. Later on you should click only when the dog nudges the ball hard enough for it to roll a short distance. When the dog nudges the ball reliably and forcefully, then leave out the action with the target wand. At this time you can instead introduce a vocal command such as *"Ball!"* or *"Roll!"*

Variation Once your dog masters the preceding lesson you can really play ball with it. Throw the ball for the dog and simultaneously give the vocal command *"Ball!"* The dog will quickly learn

to jump up at the right instant and nudge the ball hard enough for it to bounce back toward you. You have made a start if the ball comes back to you once; later on you can even do it several times in succession.

Extra Tip Here, as with all other action games, make sure that your dog does not overexert itself physically or mentally, and take regular breaks, especially in high outdoor summer temperatures. Otherwise, you risk overheating and dehydrating your dog, which can be a serious problem. Remember, your dog's welfare should always be foremost in your mind as you train it.

When the dog nudges the target wand, it automatically moves the ball. If the nudge is forceful enough, the ball will roll.

All About Retrieving

It is not uncommon for a dog to pick up and carry an object, as long as the object is of some interest to it. Certainly your dog also willingly carries its chew bone or a toy around with it from time to time. But it's a different story when you intentionally encourage the dog to retrieve. For the following exercise your dog should already have experience with the clicker.

Picking Up an Object

How It Works Use an object that the dog can pick up easily and place it on the floor. Eventually the dog will notice it. When you click depends on the dog's reaction. If at first it shows only passing interest, you should click for every glance and every step your dog makes in the direction of the object. If the dog immediately investigates, give a click as soon as it touches the item. If the dog gets heavily involved with the object, it is no longer reinforced when it merely touches it. It must now continue the experiment to find out what produces a click. If it shows that it's about to open its mouth, click. The next step would be to grasp the object—click. Then the dog must experiment further. If the dog picks it up—a click and a jackpot. Dogs that like to fetch need fewer intermediate steps, and others need more.

Possible Help Kick the object to one side if your dog initially shows little or no interest in it. That heightens the stimulation. Or hold the item in front of the dog's nose and move it back and forth. Confirm every action by the dog directed toward the object. As soon as it deliberately takes the object from your hand, train it to pick the ball up from the floor from then on. Many dogs are motivated when their owner is very busy with the object and then puts it away.

The right way to give: The dog gets a click only when it puts the ball right into your hand.

Holding On Longer

How It Works Are you wondering how your dog is supposed to learn to hold something if it gets its reward *after* dropping the item? There is a little error in thinking here. To teach a dog to hold onto an object, precise timing with the clicker is necessary. The click ends the exercise: it happens as long as the dog keeps the object in its mouth. Only then does it let go and get the reward. In no case should you click while the dog is dropping the object. At first it is acceptable if the dog holds onto the item for just a moment. Once that works reliably, click only when the dog holds on longer and gradually extends the time with greater certainty.

Extra Tip If your dog continues to hold onto the item for a fairly long time, you can have it walk at heel for a couple of minutes. It will probably learn very quickly to hold onto the item even while moving.

Giving Up the Fetched Object

How It Works Your dog will now reliably hold onto its training buck (a device used especially to train gundogs to retrieve birds) until you click. But now it should not drop it at your feet, but rather place it into your hand. Before clicking, hold your hand under the object so that it falls into your hand. Connect the release with the signal *"Give!"* or *"Thank you!"* when the dog drops the item after the click. After a few training sessions the dog will make the connection to the release signal. Now you no longer click for holding the item, but when the dog puts it into your hand upon command. If the dog drops the object without a signal, there is no click. In this case, go back a step in the exercise, for evidently the dog does not yet have a steady grasp on holding on.

1 The dog does not yet know what it is supposed to do with the ball but it tentatively moves toward it.

2 The dog understands that it is supposed to do something with the ball. It experiments further and touches it; now it gets a click.

3 But that is no longer enough. So the dog tries some more and picks up the ball in its mouth—click! One goal on the way to fetching has been met!

Fetching the Training Buck

How It Works Your dog has learned to pick up its training buck from the floor and hold onto it until you have the dog hand it over to you. Now place the object a little further away. The dog will watch while sitting or while another person holds it—then the dog is let free. It will run and pick up the object. Now move backward and encourage the dog to come to you. The dog will come to you and put the item into your hand. In the next step introduce the vocal command for fetching when the dog picks up the object—for example, *"Fetch!"* or *"Retrieve!"* When it makes the connection reliably, give the signal as soon as you send the dog after the item. When it performs the introductory exercises successfully several times, you can increase the fetching distance and continually place the object further away. The exercise is easier to control if the dog is sitting attentively next to you before you send it after the object.

Extra Tip Is your dog a passionate retriever? So, train it using different objects. Good choices for fetching are some of its toys, but also various everyday items such as a small shopping basket, a cell phone, a metal spoon, or a bunch of keys.

This dog loves to put its toy away. Placing the box right in front of the owner makes this exercise easier for the dog.

Your Dog Can Quickly Learn How to Take Things Out of a Box . . .

How It Works This exercise hardly poses any problems for a dog that can fetch.

Place a favorite fetching object in a box near you. Presumably the dog will pull it out on its own in order to bring it to you.

At first reward the dog for fetching. Once that works put several items into the box. The click now comes when the dog fetches the second object, or the third or the fourth.

If it places the items next to the box, then click while the dog is still holding them so that the item falls onto the desired spot on the floor as soon as the dog drops it; click when, for example, it turns its head in another direction or it takes a step away. Click on the behavior that is oriented in the right direction.

Once your dog understands this, don't click until it drops the item next to the box. When this exercise works, add a second object. Now click only when the second item also lies next to the box.

After several training sessions when your dog reliably takes the objects out of the box and deliberately drops them next to it, introduce the signal *"Empty the box!"* while it is picking up the object. Gradually several things will be in the box.

Possible Help If your dog is not particularly interested in the item in the box, at first replace the object with a treat and click as soon as the dog sticks its head inside the box. Usually you can eliminate the treat after a few training runs. When everything is working as desired, put the object in.

. . . and Picking Up Later

How It Works This too is a relatively easy exercise if your dog has already learned to pick up an object.

Place the box near you, and click for every movement that your dog makes in the direction of the box until it finally sticks its head into the box as if picking up. A small treat will speed up this initial procedure.

Once your dog understands the purpose of the exercise, place a familiar training buck next to the box. A dog that likes to fetch will usually pick it up spontaneously.

Let it try—if it goes to the box, or its head is already above the box—*click!* If the dog intentionally holds the fetching item over the box, don't click until the item has been placed inside the box.

When that works, you can go further. Now a second item is added. Place the object further and further away from the box.

Finally, increase the distance between you and the box. Introduce the command *"Pick up!"* when it's clear that your dog is on board with this and enjoys picking up. Give the command while the dog picks up the first object.

Possible Help Place the box right in front of you when your dog can fetch on command (see pages 37–38), and invite it to bring you its training buck. Click as soon as it drops the item into the box on the command *"Drop it."*

After a few times you can omit the command *"Drop it!"* and click as soon as the dog drops the item. Then you can also leave out *"Fetch!"*

Always click when the dog independently drops the item into the box. Once this works, place the box in different places. And when that works, add the command *"Pick up!"*

Quickly Learned: **Special Tricks**

ACTION	PERFORMANCE
HATS OFF!	Once your dog has learned to pick up a hat or a cap from the floor, it is only a small step for it to pull the item off your head. Crouch down for this. Careful: some dogs get too rambunctious!
OPEN THE DRAWER! SHUT THE DOOR!	Can the dog pick up and hold a soft, moderately thick rope? Then tie it to the handle of a drawer or a door. That way it will learn to open a drawer or shut a door.
FETCHING SPECIFIC ITEMS	Train your dog to pick up various objects and link the command *"Fetch!"* to the respective designation. That way the dog learns to bring a specific item at will. Practice this exercise separately for each object.

Little Tricks with the Paws

Dogs naturally use their forepaws for gestures of prompting and appeasement; therefore tricks with the paws are usually very easy for them.

"Paw!"

How It Works Show your dog a tasty morsel. Hold the treat in your closed hand in front of the dog. It may try at first to get to the tempting item with its muzzle, but eventually it will also use its paw—then *click!* The reward after the click comes from the other hand. At first, click even when the dog merely starts to lift its paw. As soon as it intentionally places its paw in your hand, the motivating treat can be omitted. Now introduce the command *"Paw!"*

Extra Tip If your dog puts its right paw into your left hand and the left one into your right hand, you can use the commands *"Right!"* and *"Left!"* so that it learns the difference.

"Give Me Five!"

How It Works Once your dog knows how to present a paw, it will quickly learn to give you a

This dog is a perfect master of the Spanish walk. Its mistress uses her bent right arm as a signal for it to raise its left leg.

high five. Crouch down and have the dog give you its paw several times. Start with *"Paw!"* and then leave out the command. Gradually pivot your palm until it is vertical and facing forward. Every time the dog gives you a high five—*click*. If the dog now places its paw against your hand, add the command *"High five!"*

The Spanish Walk

How It Works It is good if your dog has already learned to place its right paw into your left hand, and the left one into your right hand. Now it will learn to lift its paws as high as possible, and when it learns this thoroughly, in such a way that it no longer makes contact with your hand, but does it on command.

Gradually keep raising your hand so that the dog must also keep raising its paw higher to place it into your hand. Practice each side separately. Your dog can be either sitting or standing. The signal *"Paw!"* is used as an aid only at the beginning, then it is left out.

Eventually the dog will not place its paw in your hand, but lift it as high as possible, so always click when the paw reaches the highest point.

This can be even before the paw reaches your hand. When this works, gradually pull your hand

back as the dog lifts its paw so that it lifts the paw high in the air—*click*—without placing it into your hand.

Your raised right or left arm now becomes the signal for the appropriate side, so slightly bend right arm, left paw, and vice-versa. The other arm hangs down. Once the dog can do this equally well with both right and left paws, have it lift first one paw and then the other—*click*. Do the whole thing two or three times, and then comes the click. If you move backward at the same time and the dog follows you in the "goose-step," everything is perfect.

Once the dog reliably gives you its paw, it is a small step to the trick *"Give me five!"*

"Touch!" with the Paw

How It Works Just as you can teach your dog to touch the tip of a target wand with its nose (see pages 32–33), it can learn to use its paw for the same purpose. If you want to teach your dog to do both, it's best to use two different signals and training aids—for example, the extendable target wand for touching with the nose and a flyswatter for the paw.

Hold the swatter so that it hangs down in front of you and wait. Your dog may initially touch the swatter with its nose, especially if it has already learned this trick. But if this doesn't pan out, it may try something else and even lift a paw—*click*.

Subsequently, click every time the dog raises its paw higher or holds it near the flyswatter. Observe the dog so you immediately recognize every proper initial move.

Finally, there is one more click when the dog touches the swatter with its paw. The initially fairly brief contact between paw and flyswatter can gradually be lengthened.

As with the trick with the nose, here too you can change the position of the flyswatter and hold it further away from you or even on the floor so that the dog has to step onto it. Or hold it up so that the dog has to give it a high five (see *"Give me five!"* pages 40–41).

Possible Help Can your dog not figure out what you want it to do in this exercise? Then hold a treat under the flyswatter or place the tidbit on the ground with the flyswatter on top of it. Keep a good grip on the flyswatter.

The dog will attempt to get to the treat, perhaps at first with its muzzle. If that doesn't work, it surely will use a paw—time for a click. As soon as it understands what this is about you can leave out the treat.

This Pug has mastered the flyswatter-paw trick in all variations. The little dog even confidently places its paw on the flyswatter held high.

Human and Dog

As long as you keep a few basic points in mind with clicker training, it will be easier and quicker for your dog to reach the training goal; it will not forget what it has learned, and the fun in clicking will remain intact for both of you.

Good Idea

(+) Train only when you are relaxed and even-tempered and you have adequate time.

(+) Don't start an exercise until you understand how to reach the goal. That way your dog will also understand the individual steps.

(+) Adapt the training to the type of dog you have; some catch on quickly and are eager, and others need more time and tire more easily.

(+) Your dog should be relaxed and at its "normal" activity level. Before training, let a high-energy dog burn off a little steam.

Not So Good

(−) Never leave the clicker lying around so children and visitors are tempted to operate the "click frog."

(−) Don't react with impatience or annoyance. Your dog doesn't do anything wrong on purpose.

(−) Don't restrict your dealings with your dog to clicker training. This type of activity does not turn human and dog into a real team.

(−) Do not force your dog to perform certain behaviors through threatening body language, or by pulling on the leash in order to reinforce the actions with a click.

Shaking, Turning Around, and Walking Backward

The following exercises are fun and also are somewhat useful in daily life. Choose the ones that are most appropriate for your dog.

Shaking

How It Works Life is much easier with a dog that shakes itself on command, for example, when it returns wet from a walk, or when its fur is dirty.

Click as soon as the dog begins to shake. A dog usually shakes its fur after being brushed or when it stretches after a siesta, also when its master signals that it's time to go for a walk. And of course, whenever its fur is wet. You will be able to tell when your dog wants to shake. Keep the clicker ready. And it's the same scenario: when the dog spontaneously shakes to hear the click, introduce the command and immediately energize the action by saying *"Shake!"*

Possible Help Shaking is not an easy exercise. You may have to tickle the dog's ear or dribble a little water onto its head.

"Twist!"

How It Works For this exercise you need a treat or a target wand, in case the dog has already learned to touch the tip with its nose. The dog stands in front of you, and you hold the treat or the wand in front of its nose. How quickly you succeed depends on the dog. The goal of the exercise is for the dog to turn on its own axis, and always to the same side. Use the treat or the wand to draw a circle. Depending on the dog's responsiveness, click as soon as it moves through part of the circle. With time the click comes later. But perhaps your dog turns around like a champ right from the

It's not easy to shake on command. Many dogs need a stimulus such as water.

If the dog does not know the *"Touch!"* exercise, it can be motivated to turn on its own axis with a treat and a click.

In walking backward, crowd the dog slightly; its right hind leg makes a small movement rearward—and *click.*

beginning—*click!* As soon as it masters the turn, wait until it turns twice around the same axis before clicking. You should not ask it to do more turns than this at one stretch. Then, as usual, give the appropriate signal, such as *"Turn around!"* *"Dance!"* or *"Twist!"*

Walking Backward

How It Works Your dog stands facing you. If it happens to take a step backwards—*click.* Otherwise, crowd it slightly with your body and click when the dog starts to move backward. You can also take a step toward it, but it must not be made to feel insecure or threatened.

As soon as it reliably takes a step rearward, wait and give the click only upon the next step to the rear. For reinforcement you can again crowd the dog slightly.

Once it moves rearward several steps, introduce the signal *"Back!"* A helpful visual cue is a "stop signal" with the hand.

The goal of the exercise: the dog walks backward by itself while you remain in position.

Possible Help Begin the training in a place where the dog cannot turn to the side, but can only go rearward, for example, in a corridor. But it must not be made to feel that it is cornered.

Minis Learn to **Sit Up**

. . . AND TALL! Using the target wand or a tasty treat, smaller dogs usually learn very easily how to hunker down on their hind legs and sit up.

WALTZ KING If you combine the exercise with *"Twist!,"* your dog will turn into a perfect dancer in the twinkling of an eye.

Little Tricks for Experts

With these tricks you have a ready-made entertainment program, with signals that make people believe that the dog understands what you say.

"Take a Bow!"

How It Works Observe your dog when it "bows down" of its own accord. This may happen while stretching after a nap. This is also very typical when the dog invites you to play by lowering the front of its body. Click every time the dog adopts one of these postures. If your dog tends to lie down immediately after taking a bow, after the click take a few steps backward so that the dog will get its treat only by coming to you. During the practice, click only when the dog bows down properly, and not when it merely hints at lowering its front. When the dog bows independently, with no connection to the usual stretching or invitation to play, you can add the command *"Take a bow."*

Possible Help Is it difficult to seize the right instant for the click? Then try this: briefly hold the dog's favorite toy or a bit of food on the floor and move it as though you want to play with the dog. It will almost always answer with the desired bow—then comes the click.

"Give Me a Kiss!"

How It Works Your dog has already learned to touch the tip of the target wand (see pages 32–33). Hold the tip of the wand on your cheek and bend down to the dog. If it nudges the wand, give it a click.

Once it has practiced this successfully several times, leave out the wand and simply present your cheek to the dog. It will intentionally touch you with its nose. And as with all clicker exercises, now comes the signal for it, such as *"Give me a kiss."* For hygienic reasons, make sure that the "kissing zone" is some distance from your mouth. Kisses from high-spirited dogs can be quite rambunctious.

Possible Help If your dog is not familiar with the wand exercise, you can prepare your cheek with a dab of meat paste; then it's guaranteed that the dog will like this little trick. Gradually reduce the amount of meat paste, until the exercise works without any of the tasty persuasion.

This is what a bow looks like. Find out when your dog spontaneously bows down; that's the right time to click.

The Tired Dog

How It Works Loosely stick a small piece of cellophane tape onto one of the dog's eyebrows. It will immediately attempt to remove the foreign object with its paw—*click!* And as always, give it a reward treat. Repeat the action several times with smaller and smaller pieces of tape. Your dog will quickly realize what you want from it and will wipe its face even without cellophane tape. When it does this willingly, click only when it rubs its entire face. The signal *"Tired"* is introduced as soon as the dog directs a paw to its face.

"Yes!" and "No!"

How It Works The yes-and-no tricks should be learned one at a time so there is no confusion. First, the "yes." Hold the clicker in your hand. Your dog will look at you expectantly. Wait until it happens to look at the floor, and click as soon as its glance is directed slightly downward. It will immediately lift its head expectantly.

Again, wait until the dog looks down—*click.* Once the dog masters this, don't click until it looks straight ahead or upward. With time it will internalize the exercise and will nod its head.

You can expand the exercise by not clicking after the first nod, but rather no sooner than the second or third time. The signal can be *"Yes,"* or it can be formulated as a question: the trick is even more convincing with *"Shall we play?"* The emphasis is on *play*.

"No" functions similarly. Wait until the dog is looking to the side—*click.* When it can do this,

An easy trick: a wet dog smooch on the cheek. Adequate distance from your mouth ensures hygiene and safety for your teeth.

delay the click until the head turns back to the starting position.

When that works, click only when the head turns to the other side. Reinforce every tiny correct reaction. The signal can be *"No,"* but here too a question makes a better impression. It's especially effective with the audience if you use something that you know your dog really dislikes—for example, "Time for a bath?" Stress the word *bath*.

Possible Help Use a toy or a treat to motivate your dog to turn its head. Of course you can also use the target wand if the dog has already learned to nudge the tip.

Useful and Fun Exercises

These tricks are partly practical and partly fun, but they are not easy. With your knowledge of the clicker, however, both two- and four-legged creatures will have fun.

"Open the Door!"

How It Works If your dog is comfortable with the target wand, the following exercises will be no problem. The dog is to open a door that is not latched. Hold the target wand so that the door opens when the dog nudges the wand with its nose. At first reinforce this nudging. When the dog feels more confident, reinforce it only when it nudges the wand with enough force to open the door as wide as possible. Once the dog does this satisfactorily, the target wand is omitted. And when the exercise works reliably, add a vocal command, for example, *"Open"* or *"Open the door."* Before you start, decide if the goal of the exercise is for the door to open wider, or for the dog to open it all the way. Then work in steps to reach this goal.

Possible Help The target wand is not absolutely necessary, and the exercise can work without it. Prepare the spot on the door where the dog is to push with its nose by smearing on a dab of meat paste. Gradually use less and less of this "bait" as the dog increasingly exhibits the desired

At first the dog learns from the target wand where to push on the door to open it.

Soon the dog needs no further help. Now introduce the signal for it to open the door.

behavior. As a final and small aid, you can also rub your finger in the meat paste and help the dog to touch the door. Once your dog understands what this is about, you can even omit this help.

"Shut the Door!"

How It Works In closing the door, proceed exactly the same way as with *"Open the door,"* except that the target wand is held against the door in such a way that it closes when the dog nudges the tip. The goal: the dog should give the open door enough impetus so that it closes all the way or latches. The signal for this can be something like *"Close!"* or *"Shut the door!"*

Possible Help A little bit of meat paste on the door (see left) is an alternative to using the target wand.

Extra Tip If you want your dog to learn to open and close the door, don't start the second exercise until it masters the first one; otherwise the very similar procedures may confuse it. It doesn't matter which of the two exercises you start with.

Turning the Lights On and Off

How It Works This exercise works with a flip switch and is appropriate only for fairly large dogs that can reach the light switch. This works best when the dog is familiar with the target wand. Hold the wand horizontal with the tip on the switch. Make sure that the target wand is not in the dog's way. This exercise is a bit more difficult than *"Open/Shut the Door,"* because your dog will have to rise up to reach the switch. It will balance for a moment on its hind legs or support itself with its front paws against the wall. Since this requires some practice, you should click for the first movements in the direction of the light switch.

Turning the light on or off with a flip switch is a neat trick. Without a target wand a smudge of meat paste is a good training aid.

At first it is perfectly adequate if the dog touches the light switch. If it does so intentionally and enthusiastically, then click only when the action is strong enough for the switch to flip and turn the light on or off. With this exercise there is no distinction between turning the light on or off. A good vocal command to use is *"Light."*

Possible Help If at first it is difficult for your dog to get its bearings high up, hold the target wand below the light switch and initially just an inch or two above the dog's head. With time, the wand drifts higher until the tip eventually touches the light switch.

If your dog is not yet familiar with the target wand, you can help it in the same way as with the exercises for opening and shutting the door by first preparing the light switch with a little meat paste.

"Push!"

How about pushing a doll carriage or another small vehicle? This is a real trick, but with a little support this too will prove no problem for your dog.

How It Works Hold a treat in such a way that your dog has to place its front paws on the handle of the doll carriage in order to reach it. It gets a click for this. As soon as the dog does this willingly and promptly, move the treat a little in the direction of travel so that the dog has to push the carriage to follow the treat. Start with short stretches and gradually lengthen the distances. For a vocal command you can use *"Push."*

From **"Lie Down"** to **"Roll Over"**

PREPARATORY TRAINING It is easy to transform *"Lie down!"* into a roll-over (see page 51). The dog must not simply lie on its back but roll over to the other side.

USING THE WAND If your dog is familiar with the target wand, use it in such a way that the dog automatically rolls over when it follows the wand with its nose.

STARTING SLOWLY Click for every step. Or can your dog handle the entire roll right from the start? Gradually increase the tempo. Many dogs can do several rolls at once.

HELP FROM TREATS If your dog is not familiar with the target wand, you can use a treat to lure it into the right position. Or wait until it sponta-neously tries it from the *"Lie down!"* exercise.

Extra Tip It's a good idea to practice this exercise on a grassy area or some similar surface where the doll carriage will roll slowly. Of course you can use the target wand instead of a treat if your dog is already comfortable with this aid.

Washing the Paws

How It Works Your dog has learned to place its front paw in your hand or on a flyswatter placed on the floor. Now it must leave it there for a longer time, so don't click until the paw stays in place for a while, and gradually lengthen the time span. When the basic exercise works well, move the goal, such as the hand or the flyswatter, into a small, empty plastic basin. Once the dog partici-pates willingly, leave out the hand or the flyswatter. Once that works well, put a little water into the basin and have the dog put its paw in. With dogs that don't like water there should be just a little water on the bottom of the basin. The accompany-ing signal can be something like *"Wash!"* Dirty paws are now easy to clean up. Practice this with each paw.

Possible Help As an alternative to the flyswatter, a treat held in front of the dog's nose can be used to coax it into the basin. If it's clear that this is a major obstacle for your dog, click for small steps; for example, as soon as it lifts its paw a little.

Variation If this is not adequate, you can refine this exercise so that both forepaws are in the basin at the same time. When the dog places one paw securely into the empty basin, stop clicking. Now it generally will try various things. Pay close attention to every tiny movement in the right direction! As soon as it moves the other forepaw, even a tiny bit, give it a click. Click for even minimal progress.

This Pug has placed its paw onto the wand and stands with one leg in the filled basin. This paw is ready to be wiped off.

If you want, you can teach your dog to stand in the basin with all four paws; for example, by having the dog follow the wand with its nose and stepping into the basin.

Perhaps your dog is really crafty and puts its second leg into the basin quicker than you had expected. Then it still has to learn to stand calmly for a fairly long time.

"On Your Back!"

How It Works The goal of this training session: getting your dog to lie on its back. This has a number of practical advantages. Among others, you can clean its underside or remove a tick from this area. Observe your dog—does it like to roll frequently in the grass or on a rug? Click as soon as it has all four feet in the air. Does it exhibit this behavior on its own, perhaps after a practice session? Then

delay the click. Your dog should remain calmly in this position. Then you can click. Gradually increase the time, and eventually introduce the signal, such as *"On your back!"* We always tell our dog *"Tummy!"*

Possible Help If your dog obeys the command *"Down!"* hold a treat in front of its nose and move it so that the dog has to roll onto its back to follow the treat with its eyes. Click as soon as the body turns in the required direction, rather than when the dog is lying entirely on its back.

Extra Tip Many dogs, especially ones that are insecure, don't like to lie on their back. These dogs should be excused from the exercise.

Help with Problems

A clicker is a wonderful aid in teaching things to dogs, but as with all methods of dog training, it is not a cure-all. In order to keep the fun intact you will now learn how to avoid problems and what is important in using the clicker.

If Your Dog Doesn't Want to Cooperate

For most dogs the clicker quickly becomes a real highlight, but with others it can take some time for things to sink in and for the dog to come to grips with clicker training.

Fear of the Click

Some dogs are afraid of the clicking noise, but if your dog is not overly fearful in other situations, it soon will learn to appreciate the positive sides of the clicker and get used to the click.

In order to work with a dog that is particularly sensitive to noises, you can slightly muffle the sound of the click. Either hold the clicker behind your back or activate it inside the pocket of your jacket or pants.

› If the dog proves so sensitive that it doesn't even take a treat or wants to run away, the conditioning must first be interrupted. Now the main thing is to convince the dog that the clicker poses no danger to it. This is easiest to achieve when your dog experiences something particularly positive, for example, it is served its favorite food, or when you play with it and throw the ball for it. Click immediately before each action but keep an adequate distance from the dog, or muffle the clicker so that the dog does not immediately react defensively.

› Unfortunately, even this preparatory training does not work with many dogs. In this case the clicker should no longer be used. Instead, think of an exclusive word with a particular inflection and condition your dog to it.

Passive Behavior

Your dog has been properly conditioned and understands the connection between the click and the treat given as a reward—and yet it shows no inclination to try anything in the framework of the exercise.

Cross-over Problem The causes of the passive behavior may lie in the type of training. If negative reinforcement or positive punishment are used primarily, this training technique very likely has decisively inhibited the dog's initiative. The dog must have experienced that there are negative conse-

quences when it spontaneously becomes active; therefore, it ceases the independent behavior. This is referred to as a cross-over problem.

A Mixture of Praise and Negative Reinforcement Even mixed forms of training based on praise or force can produce passiveness. But this is not generally true and can even result from the dog's sensitivity and from the intensity and the frequency of the negative reinforcement used.

Fixation Initial comprehension problems may also result if the dog has been trained in a particular area and is fixated on it; for example, on tracking or retrieving. If you now begin with a new clicker exercise and practice a trick that is different from everything that the dog has leaned previously, it may be beyond the dog. Often the result is a lack of initiative.

Be Patient! Don't throw in the towel right away. Try to tempt your dog into doing even a small movement and click right when it flicks an ear. With a little patience the dog often will acquire a taste for it on its own. If you used force before starting with clicker training, you must avoid falling back into the old pattern. Forgo any verbal-, body language-, or physical correction if the dog doesn't do what you expect of it.

No Appetite

Does your dog have no interest in treats? Could your dog be too full? Cut back on the meal or leave out one or two meals; often this is all it takes to

If you actuate the clicker in your pants pocket, the noise is muffled. This is a help to sensitive dogs.

If a dog is insecure because of severe training or by nature, clicking may cause problems: the dog doesn't have the confidence to become active.

With enthusiasm for clicker training, keep your dog from turning into an overstimulated clicker junkie. Quality comes before quantity.

pique interest. Or does the dog always get treats for no reason? Correct that situation. From now on the dog gets treats only in conjunction with clicking. If your dog is very finicky—if it likes one type on one occasion and then no more—you should change the type of treats more frequently, and before the dog scorns them. If that doesn't help, then find out what it likes to eat, even the widest varieties of sausages and cheeses, fruit, vegetables—and things that you don't find particularly appealing, such as dried fish and raw pieces of beef. Many dogs refuse to eat when they are distracted. Provide calm surroundings free from distractions. Very fearful dogs may also refuse treats. Choose a setting for the training where your dog feels more secure.

Frantic Behavior

Is your dog over-excited, nervous, and distracted in clicker training? Then perhaps you have done

too much or have gone too quickly. Take a fairly long break or in the coming time practice calm behavior. Above all, it's important for you to remain calm and relaxed and refuse to approve the frantic behavior.

Demand Respect from Your Dog

YOU ARE THE BOSS In the human-dog team, you are the dominant partner, and the dog should orient itself toward you in everyday situations, not the other way around!

A GOOD RELATIONSHIP Togetherness works only when the dog takes you seriously and respects you—with or without a clicker.

The Right Way to Correct Bad Behavior

Now you have experienced it yourself through the exercises presented—the clicker is great for reinforcing desirable behavior in your dog, and it helps the dog learn even complex behaviors relatively easily and securely. But what can you do if you have accidentally reinforced the wrong thing or the dog displays habits that must be broken?

When You Reinforce the Wrong Thing

If your timing is wrong and you have repeatedly clicked at the wrong instant, your dog has learned something wrong; for example, you want to reinforce eye contact, but you click just a tad late several times. The result: the dog has already broken eye contact and is looking away. Subsequently, it will continue to look away.

The same applies to holding tight to a fetching buck: if you click too late, when the dog is no longer holding on tightly, it learns that click means to drop it.

> The dog often reacts so quickly that you don't always catch the right instant for the click. It's not the end of the world—as soon as you realize your mistake, simply stop reinforcing the behavior. If you are consistent, your dog will stop doing it after a while.

Since the stimulus is absent, there's nothing in it for the dog, and it won't waste any more energy on it. If the undesirable connection has taken hold, the behavior still can appear temporarily reinforced. Persevere, and start the exercise again when the behavior has subsided.

> Change the training when a step of a complex exercise no longer comes off properly. Practice this individual step separately and as long as it takes for it to work properly. Only then does the entire exercise return to the training program.

With a dog that jumps up the clicker is not the means of choice. Turning away and ignoring the dog are called for.

Breaking a Dog of Bad Behavior

The clicker has its limits with bad behavior by a dog. You can reinforce desirable behavior, but not break bad behavior. In many cases, however, you can set up an alternative behavior.

For example, if the dog races to the door every time the doorbell rings, you can instead reinforce the behavior of lying in its bed upon your signal. At first, reinforce this outside the context of the doorbell. When the dog masters this, reinforce it when the bell rings, and, finally, in conjunction with the ringing and the arrival of visitors (who of course should ignore the dog).

Self-rewarding Behavior Many types of behavior motivate the dog during the actions themselves. They exert a stimulus on it that a reward cannot counter. The dog practically rewards itself.

A typical example is the will to hunt. You may be able to establish an alternative behavior right at the start of a hunting sequence, but generally that works only with a reduced passion for hunting and a highly trainable dog, and not with a pronounced urge to hunt.

The situation is similar when your dog continually looks for edibles or rolls in filth while on a walk, or gnaws on electric wires or the carpet. Here the clicker is of no further use. In such cases, you will not manage without a conditioned stop signal. An unpleasant action is connected to an audible signal. Good signals are *"No!"* or *"Stop!"* or rattling a stone-filled can.

In order to be effective, you have to know your dog's reactions precisely. The effect must not be

Wrong reinforcement: on a walk the dog remains standing, you tempt it with a treat, and thus reward it for remaining standing.

too mild or too strong—it must cause the dog to cease the behavior it has just begun.

Once the dog connects the effect and the signal, the signal by itself will suffice. The effect or the signal must occur right at the start of the bad behavior, not when the desired action is already underway. When the dog stops the bad behavior, require an alternative behavior and reward it.

Avoiding Lapses When the dog is alone and steps out of line, clicker training is of no help. Does it sleep on the sofa or steal food from the table? Then you have to make future lapses impossible, or at least difficult. With a sofa sleeper, the door to the living room is henceforth closed, and all foods moved out of reach of a food thief.

Improper Use of the Clicker

In using the clicker it is possible to do something wrong. Specifically there is a tempting source of error that leads to a lack of success with clicker training, or at least to results other than the desired ones.

After Conditioning

Many dog owners use the clicker to attract their dog's attention if it does not come when called or is otherwise distracted. At first, this usually works well. When the dog hears the familiar sound, after being conditioned to the clicker, it surely will react and come to get a treat. So evidently the click worked. But watch out—this is an error in reasoning. With this use of the clicker, the dog learns that its behavior just before the click was right, so if you click because your dog ignores the *"Come!"* command, and instead keeps digging for mice, you ultimately reinforce this undesirable behavior. Here's another common case: Your dog pulls on

No stealing from the table! Firm rules and limits and their consistent enforcement, along with learning signals, are essential. Then life together works fine.

the leash because it wants to run after a jogger instead of concentrating on you. If you click now, the dog surely will look up at you and get its reward, but for the dog this is a confirmation for its "thrill of the chase" for the jogger, not the eye contact with you. You must click while the dog is looking at you, and in no case before that happens.

Prior to Conditioning

If you use the clicker to get your dog's attention, this will also work before the dog is conditioned to it. The unaccustomed clicking piques the dog's curiosity, and it will want to find the source of the noise. Eventually it will become familiar with the noise, and it will lose its appeal or the dog will react to it only when it has nothing better to do. Ultimately the clicker will have no meaning for the dog, and you will no longer be able to use it successfully.

No Substitute for the Proper Procedure

Many first-time users are stunned at how easy it is to teach their dog by using a clicker, but don't forget: the dog is no machine, and the clicker is no cure-all. A harmonious life together requires more than a connection through a click. The most important things are a trusting relationship and the owner's confident demeanor, so that the dog accepts and respects the person as the team leader. A dog must learn and comply with the rules for living together. It is thus important that everyone involved treat the dog in a consistent manner.

The Limits of the Clicker

TIPS FROM THE
CLICKER EXPERT

INBORN CHARACTERISTICS A dog that is naturally fearful and insecure with respect to either humans or other influences cannot be "cured" through clicker training. It is not possible to influence genetics. Even deficits in socialization can rarely be corrected, especially with an inborn, unstable bundle of nerves. The case is similar for breed-typical qualities such as pronounced instincts for guarding and protection, a passion for hunting, and so forth. If you cannot deal with a problem you should get competent help in a timely fashion.

RESEARCH INTO CAUSES Many times it is recommended to bring problem behaviors under signal control—that is, to teach the dog not to do something without a command. Jumping up on people, continuous barking, restless behavior, and so forth, may be due to a variety of causes, such as inadequate mental engagement, stress, mistrust, and unconscious rewarding. In such cases it makes more sense to first discover the cause and treat it, rather than merely the symptoms.

Clubs / Associations

> American Kennel Club
5880 Centerview Drive, Suite 200
Raleigh, NC 27606-3390
919-233-9780

> The Canadian Kennel Club
100-89 Skyway Avenue
Etobicoke, Ontario M96R4
Canada
416-675-5511

> American Rare Breeds
   Association
9921 Frank Tippett Road
Cheltenham, MD 20623
301-868-5718

> United Kennel Club
100 E. Kilgore Road
Kalamazoo, MI 49002-5584
515-343-9020

*You can get the addresses for dog
clubs and associations from the
foregoing contacts.*

Questions on Dog Ownership

Check with your pet shop owner,
your veterinarian, and online. The
addresses above also provide
useful information.

Insurance

Check with your insurance company;
some offer liability insurance for
dog owners, and even health insurance for pets. Some veterinarians
have brochures and other information about insurance.

Dog Registry

You can protect your dog from animal thieves and death in a research
laboratory by entering it into a
dog registry. Entry and computer-
assisted search upon report of a
missing dog are free.

Dogs on the Internet

> **www.dogbreedinfo.com**
(information on specific breeds)
> **www.akc.org/clubs/search/
index.cfm** (find a dog club based
on the type of training, services, and
competition that the club provides)
> **www.servicedogcentral.org/
content/** (a site for dog service
partners and trainers)
> **www.gopetsamerica.com/
dog-good-with-kids.aspx** (breeds
that are commonly recommended
as being compatible with children)
> **http://dog.about.com/od/
healthandwellness/Health.htm**
(information about canine health,
problems, and care)
> **http://www.pupdogtraining.com**
(train a dog at home like a pro)

Books

> Alderton, David. *The Dog Selector.*
Hauppauge, New York: Barron's
Educational Series, Inc., 2010.
> American Kennel Club. *The
Complete Dog Book.* New York, New
York: Howell Book House, 1992.
> Ammen, Amy. *Training in No Time:
An Expert's Approach to Effective
Dog Training for Hectic Life Styles.*
New York, New York: Howell Book
House, 1995.
> Ludwig, Gerd. *Sit! Stay! Train
Your Dog the Easy Way, 2nd ed.,*
Hauppauge, New York: Barron's
Educational Series, Inc., 2008.
> Taunton, Stephanie J. and Cheryl
S. Smith. *The Trick Is in the Training,
2nd ed.* Hauppauge, New York:
Barron's Educational Series, Inc.,
2010.
> Tennant, Colin. *Dog Training &
Behavior, 2nd ed.* Hauppauge, New
York: Barron's Educational Series,
Inc., 2005.

Magazines

> *AKC Gazette*
Subscriptions: 919-233-9767
> *Dog Fancy*
P.O. Box 53264
Boulder, CO 80322-3264
> *Dog World*
29 North Wacker Drive
Chicago, IL 60606
> *Off-Lead*
204 Lewis Street
Canastota, NY 13032
800-241-7619

First edition translated from the German by Eric A. Bye.

English translation © copyright 2011 by Barron's Educational Series, Inc.

Original title of the book in German is *Hunde—Clickertraining*.

© copyright 2009 by Gräfe und Unzer Verlag GmbH, Munich.

All inquiries should be addressed to:
Barron's Educational Series, Inc.
250 Wireless Boulevard
Hauppauge, NY 11788
www.barronseduc.com

ISBN-13: 978-0-7641-4577-3
ISBN-10: 0-7641-4577-0

Library of Congress Catalog Card No.: 2010026832

Library of Congress Cataloging-in-Publication Data
Schlegl-Kofler, Katharina.
    [Hunde—Clickertraining. English]
    Clicker training / Katharina Schlegl-Kofler ; translated from the German by Eric A. Bye. — 1st ed.
        p. cm.
    Includes bibliographical references and index.
    ISBN-13: 978-0-7641-4577-3
    ISBN-10: 0-7641-4577-0
1. Dogs—Training. 2. Clicker training (Animal training). I. Title.
SF431.S34513 2011
636.7'0835—dc22   2010026832

Printed in China
9 8 7 6 5 4 3 2 1

The Author

Katharina Schlegl-Kofler—an experienced dog trainer and a recognized expert in proper dog ownership—has long been deeply involved with dogs and their behavior. In her dog school, which she has had for four years, dog owners find enthusiastic help. She has owned a Labrador Retriever for a long time.

The Photographers

Oliver Giel specializes in nature and animal photography, and with his companion Eva Scherer he provides photos for books, periodicals, calendars, and advertising. You can learn more about his photo studio at www.tierfotograf.com.

Christine Steimer is a freelance photographer and specializes in pet photography. She works for international book publishers, specialized periodicals, and advertising agencies.

All photos in this book are from Oliver Giel, except for: Christine Steimer: 2–2, 3, 15, 29, 30, 32, 33, 35, 39, 44, 45, 46, 47, 55, 56, and 57

SOS – What to Do?

Clicking with Two Dogs

PROBLEM You want to train two dogs. **THIS MAY HELP** At first, condition each dog individually and go through the first exercises separately. Later on, the dogs will distinguish which one the click is for.

Too Old?

PROBLEM Your dog has physical problems or is old. **THIS MAY HELP** Neither of these excludes the possibility of clicker training. On the contrary: with arthritis or other restrictions to agility, calm exercises using the wits are very beneficial. The dog keeps busy without being overworked.

Negligence in Training

PROBLEM An exercise is performed with ever-decreasing precision. **THIS MAY HELP** Go back a few steps. Perhaps you structured the exercise too hastily, or reinforced inadequately precise performances too frequently. It is helpful to take a break from the clicker for a couple of days.

Food Allergy

PROBLEM Your dog can hardly get any treats because it is allergic to practically everything. **THIS MAY HELP** First talk with your veterinarian; he or she may be able to help you solve the problem. Many manufacturers of hypoallergic foods also offer appropriate treats. Of course you can also use dry food nuggets that meet these special requirements. If your dog cannot tolerate beef, lamb, or chicken in its food, you should try horse meat. Also, boiled potatoes are generally good for dogs with allergies, and most dogs like the taste.

Insecurity

PROBLEM The dog is fearful and unreceptive. **THIS MAY HELP** If the fear is pronounced, temporarily giving a tranquilizer may help in allowing general access to the dog, regardless of whether or not you wish to work with the clicker. Consult with your veterinarian about the problem.